WILL THERE BE A SUNSET?

CHICKEN HOUSE PRESS

More are men's ends mark'd than their lives before:
The setting sun, and music at the close,
As the last test of sweets, is sweetest last,
Writ in remembrance more than things long past

William Shakespeare

CONTENTS

FOREWORD

Will There Be a Sunset?

Pause.

The theme of this anthology brings many possibilities to mind:

Survival and hope? Aging and mortality as we head to our final days? A romantic relationship gone right?

A sunset brings to mind photographs and paintings and careful brushstrokes...

When I was selected as the judge for the eight finalists, I eagerly anticipated the offerings. I wasn't disappointed...

Rewind.

A few years ago, I was one of the writers submitting to the very first contest offered by Chicken House Press. The theme for that challenge was "The Things We Leave Behind," and my winning story, "Menos Coca, Más Cacao" (Less Cocaine, More Cocoa) opened up quite a few doors for me.

It's a story I'm proud of, to be sure, tied with another, "The Killing Jar," as my best ever, I think.

First, it was published with the short stories of the other seven finalists in an anthology by the same title, *The Things We Leave Behind*. When I received my copy, I was able to read the other stories fully and learn from their craft.

Part of the prize back then involved a manuscript review to see if I had a body of work worth publishing. After getting rid of one story that clearly didn't fit and adding another, Chicken House Press and Alanna Rusnak published *How to Make a Killing Jar*, a collection of 12+1 of my short stories, in August of 2023.

The attention I got from the contest and the book led to me being a presenter at the Surrey International Writers Conference this past October.

It also led to the opportunity for me to be a judge in what is the third contest now for Chicken House Press: *Will There Be a Sunset?*

Play.

I received the batch of eight stories, and what did I find?

Strong down-home voices and a feline point of view. Britney Spears and AC/DC and other 80's nostalgia... in 2004. The art of advertising... and murder. One writer takes us far into the future and the Dream Forecasting Institute. Another makes us deeply feel a mother's grief and regret.

And the two winners? Mysteriously, they both use dandelions symbolically to connect to theme and motif, telling tales that will stay with readers long after they put this book down. They also use plenty of tools and writing craft to make images stick in the brain.

Let's get to the stories and their writers. I'll start with the winner and the runner-up, then address the other six stories in order of author last name.

"Golden," by Juliette Willows, is a standout winner. The title, "Golden," obviously connects to the contest theme. In this story, there is an older couple in the sunset years of their relationship and their lives. There is a pair of cardinals, red birds to represent the two of them, red to connect to many sunsets together and their love for each other. Yellow comes through in the dandelion honey she makes for him, at first, then the batches of it they make together, and finally, the jars he fills on his own when she is no longer able to.

Sometimes the yellow comes through in beautiful imagery: "She relaxes into the new cushion he gifted her... It's the palest shade of buttery yellow—her favourite colour—embroidered with a dusting of tiny daisies. It reminds him of the colour she'd chosen to paint the kitchen... The paint had faded, along with the grief, over the years."

I loved the organization of this piece as well. The writer uses the seasons—winter, spring, summer, and autumn—in that order, to frame the story. Also, there is a bit of a refrain at the beginning of each section. Read the opening lines about day and night in each of the four parts and you will find sentences separated by sections that combine together to create a unified whole. They act like echoes, and a wide variety of sound devices are employed, along with fluency techniques, to make it a pleasure to read aloud.

What is most beautiful is how all elements combine to connect to the theme. The strong, connotative language, deep symbolism, and detailed imagery make this story a work of art!

Speaking of works of art, Ronald Zajac's runner-up story, "Dandelion Seeds," centres around a mural that some of his art students have put up in a public space illegally at night. They are willing to risk it all for art, for ideas that are important to them.

The protagonist—their teacher—Patrick Morrow, photographs and paints sunsets. He may be in the sunset of his own career too, he realizes, as he is currently struggling with his craft while he watches younger artists come to the forefront to take his place. His health is suffering, so he may be rapidly approaching his own sunset too.

The mural integrates the image of a BIPOC woman blowing seeds from a dandelion into the sky. The yellow dandelion, now white, has reached the sunset of its own life, but the seeds are free to create life anew. The image connects not only to the teacher, but also to a student from his college, Lily Feng. She has had her own journey, one involving racism and hate. The mural, she feels, is her:

"She is a dandelion seed floating higher than any seed has ever been lifted, and right now she can choose which way the wind blows her."

Patrick's story and Lily's story intersect in the most beautiful way. As one learns to appreciate sunset moments, the other sees a sunrise of her life.

It is this strong, deep integration of the theme and careful writing craft that made Willows' and Zajac's stories my top two selections.

Let's look at some golden rays from the other six stories:

Anne Baldo's story, "When Britney Spears Comes on the Radio," shows the importance of detail in establishing setting. We read, in the fifth paragraph, that we are in 2004, but the characters are clearly stuck in the 80s and 90s: AC/DC, purple eyeshadow, Britney Spears and Usher, chokers, heart-shaped lockets, and *Curious* perfume. The desire to be something other than what they are? The push to pursue a more passionate relationship? Double standards and unrequited love? Baldo's tale brings to the forefront these emotional issues and more, like body image and societal expectations:

"Claire is right; she usually is. She has a lot of rules and she prefers when we follow them too, like never wearing lip liner without lipstick or how you don't let guys grind you on the dance floor and that I am not supposed to talk to Asher ever again or even think about him anymore, and the last one is probably true."

It's the voice of an 18-year-old under attack from all sides. The choices she makes and does not make in her relationships ultimately connect to her personal thoughts about the opening line:

"We are always okay or we say we're okay and for years we believe this is the same thing."

At the very beginning of Gary Kirchner's "Wolverine," readers know they are in for a fun ride told through feline eyes:

"Don't think like a tabby," he would scold me. "Think of the most vicious animal you can. Lioness, tigress, whatever. *Become* it."

Just like that, we are in the mind of a four-footed furry creature who's attempting to establish some swagger. We follow her as she steals fish, defends her treasure, fights for those she believes in, and yes, even kills. We see life on the streets in a way we never have, yet with echoes that are vaguely familiar.

It's an allegory with an aggressive attitude:

"They killed my brother...that's when I became a wolverine."

In "Alienation," Barbara Lehtiniemi follows the age-old

advice of not having all your characters sound like you.

When Jake speaks, we can make immediate judgements, right or wrong, about his attitude and education: "I was already swingin' the bat before I was even proper awake."

Alberta is more refined and contemplative: "I shouldn't have meddled with his mind... I see that now. I see a lot now."

The difference in voice shows readers another possibility—the opportunity for one to easily manipulate the other. But just because something is possible, doesn't mean it should be done. The decision to act on that personal power, to use influence as a tool, as a weapon, leads to tragedy in this tale. Ultimately, it is the voices that make it believable.

In our current push for more and more AI-assisted living, Chris Meyer's "Lucid Observer" is a timely commentary on where we may be headed in the not-so-distant future. Perhaps one of our greatest fears is that one day we will succumb to technology, that it will outsmart us all, that it will reach a state where it has no need for us.

In this story, Meyer manages to include cli-fi elements as well. As we continue to pollute the Earth, it will ultimately become unlivable. What then? A rush to find somewhere we can breathe easily? And who might be competing for those valuable spots? Desperation speaks in the details:

"The mob's voices have merged into a throbbing groan of desperation, and the stale air among them is suffocating."

But another conundrum surfaces in this AI-infected world: How do we tell what is a real threat, and what is manufactured or molded into something more palatable?

Cheryl Skory Suma uses the motif of a ticking clock to explore existentialist ideas in "Minutes Lost in Death's Doubt & Other Unplanned Sunsets." We think of life as a slow, gradual aging process, but time can be altered with one quick diagnosis, with one quick word:

"Cancer."

In her story, an overwhelming message involving valuing the time we do have comes through clearly. This is especially true during the protagonist's darkest moment:

"My brand of cancer...one I'd never heard of before. The kind that drove my doctor to look carefully over my shoulder as he talked. The kind that made him say you should get your affairs in order... The minute-counting kind."

Her skillful use of repetition and hard-hitting descriptions make readers experience the pain themselves, but may ultimately lead to enjoying the life we have that much more.

Another writer who is skilled in conveying these deep emotions is Liz Torlée in her story, "Flight." The deep regret and grief of her character is evident early on, in the very first line:

"I'm wearing a grey wig to my baby daughter's funeral so no one will recognize me."

Again, the ability to make the pain palpable to readers is evident in the detailed imagery:

"The lake stared back, a fiery orange bleeding along the horizon... My breath stuck in the back of my throat."

In describing what is every parent's nightmare, Torlée makes us understand the depth of hurt and the desire for disappearance, a new beginning.

The stories in this anthology do indeed include brilliant sunsets, stark photographs, and detailed paintings. The imagery will make characters, settings, and plots live inside your mind. Better yet? You might be inspired to write your own story, to include your own beautiful brushstrokes, and to enter the NEXT contest sponsored by Chicken House Press. I wish you a pleasant experience putting pen to paper, fingers to keyboard!

Fast forward!

Ace Baker
author of *How to Make a Killing Jar*

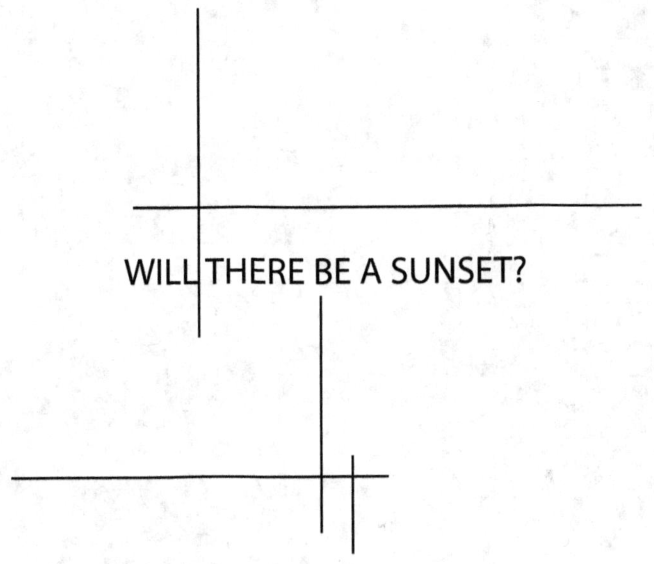
WILL THERE BE A SUNSET?

GOLDEN

Juliette Willows

Winter

THE DAYS ARE SHORT. NIGHTS, LONG, FRIGID, etching frosty road maps on the windowpanes. Bones catch chill easily, brittle as the crackling logs on the hearth, snapping with every lick of the dancing flame, keeping Father Winter at bay.

The old man smiles, though the dull ache in his knees reminds him of the season with every small push of the rocker.

He knows every soft sound like he knows the resonance of his own breathing—short and shallow these days, quickly winded, especially in the icy air beyond the door.

Though his body betrays him, as of late, his hearing

remains sharp now, as it was a lifetime ago, half a world away, lying in muddy barracks among brothers and comrades.

The kettle begins to blow its increasing whistle and he counts, one, two, three, and the whistle stops. Always three, not a second less, not one longer. The low gurgle of the boiling water over the Earl Grey tea leaves, soft squeeze of the tangerine wedge for a splash of citrus—he hates lemon. The melodic clinking of the dainty, perfectly polished silver spoon on bone china as she stirs in half a spoonful of dandelion honey.

He'll only have her dandelion honey—none other. He picks the blooms for her, in the spring and again in autumn. An inch of stem, just exactly; no leaves, no roots, then he watches as she weaves her magic. An old family recipe, to be followed just so. A hundred turns to the left, seventy-five to the right, with the wooden spoon handed down from her grandmother, and hers before. Stained and worn smooth by time and many loving hands.

A flutter of scarlet at the window catches his eye as the languid shuffle on worn hardwood approaches. Another flutter, not quite so bright, joins the first as she reaches him, lowering his cup and saucer to the small table between their twin chairs.

Quietly, she sits by him, picking up her knitting from the small basket at her feet. Another pair of tiny socks he'll add to the ever-growing collection in the large trunk at the foot of their bed. More than sixty years, she's been knitting them, and he's been storing them. Every minuscule pair, lovingly stitched, meticulously wrapped in white tissue paper and carefully placed with the others.

He doesn't have the heart to tell her she's running out of space. Doesn't have the heart to tell her it still breaks him every time—remembering the pain, the despair of those moments so many decades ago. The tiny child. Too small, too early. Much too early. Much too weak...

There weren't any others after that. Her body had been as broken as her heart and couldn't carry another life. So, she'd shut herself away with her knitting needles, and never stopped.

The movement at the window catches her eye as she looks up from her work, smiles, turns to him and smiles more brightly still, and for the first time, he sees it. A slight haze clouding the deep blue pools he'd fallen in love with a lifetime ago. A faint tremor in her slender hands. He smiles back as the bright red cardinals peck at the seeds on the frozen windowsill, reaches for her hand in the space between them, rubs the pad of his thumb across her frail knuckles.

The day ends early this time of year, and they sit and watch the cardinals fly off as the sun dips beneath the frozen landscape, behind an evergreen canvas in an otherwise monochrome world.

Spring

The days are getting longer now, nights, shorter, though still crisp, fresh on the skin, through the open windows. The etchings of winter's story have finally faded from the tempered panes, replaced by the mirage of rainbows against the glass. The silver sky of winter, transposed by the bright blue of spring, soft, cerulean sweeps painted across the horizon, broad strokes of white, watercolour clouds like lace on a young bride's veil.

He recalls standing at the front of the little white church, watching his own bride, many years past, walking on her father's arm towards him. Step by measured step along the threadbare, mustard yellow carpet of the aisle. The hushed gasps of their friends and loved ones from the polished pews —she had eyes only for him, as tears flowed freely down the rosy apples of her flushed cheeks. The flowing, strawberry blonde tresses looped in a long, flowered braid over her shoulder, studded with pink rosebuds and baby's-breath. How lovely she looked that day. How lovely that night—the night that would lead to such heartbreak less than eight months later.

Just as lovely now, he thinks, as she watches her hands lower his cup to the table with a tremor. It's no longer possible for her to conceal it, and his heart squeezes like a fist as he sees the sorrow hiding behind her smile.

She sits, holding her knitting against her chest as though it were a cherished treasure, her eyes following the crimson flutter at the window. A deep, shuddering breath lifts her shoulders before she relaxes into the new cushion he gifted her, seeing how the wood of the chair bruises her fragile body.

It's the palest shade of buttery yellow—her favourite colour—embroidered with a dusting of tiny daisies. It reminds him of the colour she'd chosen to paint the kitchen when he'd first bought her this house, the week after they were wed. It was a happy colour, she'd insisted, when he'd come home from the war to find her baking his favourite cake to celebrate his return, her belly swollen to nearly bursting.

The paint had faded, along with the grief, over the years. Bleached by the sun pouring into the big windows, just as the strawberry blonde of her hair had slowly turned to silver, then the beautiful, snowy white it was today.

She'd run her hand lovingly over the soft fabric when she'd pulled it from the gift box. Her smile had radiated joy, bringing him back to their youth for a brief moment.

She barely stitches together a row or two before setting her work back into her lap, feigning not being in the mood to knit, as the cardinals peck at sunflower seeds and corn kernels on the windowsill. A tired smile lifts the corners of her lips as she watches the nightly ritual.

The old man frowns, worry creasing his brow; she's never not in the knitting mood. They sit for a long while, watching as the cardinals fly off to their new nest in the blooming cherry blossoms by the fence, and the red sun sits low on the greening horizon, casting coral hues across the western sky as it sinks into the Pacific Ocean.

Summer

The days are long. Nights, short, sweltering, leaving trickling moisture on the window panes. Sweat sticks to skin, folding in every crease. No chill to catch now, but the heat steals breath from lungs like a bandit in the night, and he almost wishes for winter again. Almost.

He remembers the extremes of the barracks. The oppressive heat that clung to every surface in a relentless blanket of dampness. The constant buzz of insects, day and night—though mostly noticeable at night, when the jungle closed in on them, obliterating any semblance of light. The only thing that had kept him going, then, was the thought of her in this little house, waiting for him, their child in her growing womb. Her photo tucked into his breast pocket, along with a perpetually crushed packet of cigarettes, was his lifeline then, as her presence beside him is now.

The old man smiles, though his smile is sad, as he recalls the earlier hours of the day; the air in the small yellow kitchen, sticky sweet with the scent of nectar syrup growing thicker with every turn. Her hands, too weak and unsteady to hold the spoon, folded into silent prayer as she watched him stir.

She counted for him, out loud, although her voice was but a whisper, from her perch on the kitchen chair he pulled up for her. He counted along with her, silently in his head, as she long ago lost count and momentarily forgot what they were doing. A hundred to the left, seventy-five to the right.

He smiled at her as he dipped a finger into the steaming pot, coating it with the buttery yellow concoction and bringing it to her lips for a taste.

They sit now, watching the red feathery pair feast on the seeds he's scattered for them on the windowsill, ever constant as the needles on the clock. The male catches the old man's gaze, holds it; his small head tilted to the side as though in silent conversation while his mate tires, sits on the ledge, quietly waiting. A strange knowing passes from creature to man, from man to creature.

The steaming cups of tea between them don't taste quite right; he brewed them, as she can't seem to remember how to boil the water or measure the leaves. That morning, she'd forgotten what the dandelions were called, and had started to cry.

He'd dried her tears with the handkerchief she'd sewn for him, before pulling up the chair by the stove. Their cardinal friends had joined them, then, at the open kitchen window, with a sweet serenade that made her smile again.

The knitting sits untouched at her feet as she rocks slowly back and forth, observing the scene, vacantly, as her tea grows tepid. She tips her head to the side, turning towards him, her mouth slightly open as though she's about to speak, but then thinks better of it, or, more likely, forgets what she was about to say, and turns back to the window with a quivering lip.

Silently, he grasps her hand in the space between them, holding the delicate fingers in his as the bright orange ball drops low in a sun-kissed sky. It takes its time, going slowly, as though trying to make this moment last.

The old man sighs deeply as the last sliver of fiery light dips below the deep blue surf, just as his bride nods off to sleep in the chair beside him, her hand going limp in his grasp.

Autumn

The days are growing short again. Nights, quiet, lonely, weaving dreams into nightmares. Blind to the beauty of nature's canvas, he wipes the trail of tears from his leathery cheeks.

His tea sits on the table beside him, cooled and untouched. On the window ledge, the male cardinal sits quietly with him, as though he knows. *He probably does,* the old man thinks, as he hasn't seen the scarlet critter's companion in weeks, and he's sat in the cherry tree for hours every day, calling out a heartbreaking song with no response.

The small, woven basket sits beneath the window, cashmere-soft, powder blue yarn spilling in mounds over the edge, a pair of old, slightly bent knitting needles standing like tired sentinels in wait. She never did finish that last pair of tiny socks. She'd even asked him, near the end, what it was he kept in that basket.

His heart had broken then, all over again, though at the same time, he'd felt relief for her. For the first time in more than six decades, she didn't know the grief she'd carried her entire life. Didn't remember the loss, the pain, the heartache. He supposed there was a silver lining in the dark clouds hovering over her.

Silently, on a long-suffering sigh, he stands, shuffles to the little kitchen, and pours the cold tea down the sink, placing the rinsed, empty cup on the rack to dry. He walks through every room, taking a long look at a lifetime of memories.

The faded yellow paint on the kitchen walls. The sepia-toned framed photo of their wedding, hanging above the brick fireplace, his bride's pretty smile turned to him. The daisy cushion, the untouched knitting, the trunk full of tiny socks, the perfectly pressed army-greens hanging in the back of the bedroom closet. A simple life, it's been, but he wouldn't have traded a moment of it. Not the love, nor the hurt.

On tired legs, he steps out onto the front porch, closing the door softly behind him. The air is fresh, scented sweetly with the decay of the brightly coloured leaves carpeting the expanse of grass he's allowed to grow too tall. No matter, now. He breathes it in, as deeply as his lungs will allow, as he tips his face up to the evening sky.

For decades, he's sat in that front window with the love of his life, drinking dandelion honey tea, watching the sun set past the fields, the never-ending expanse of evergreens, into the depths of the Pacific, where the snow-tipped mountains wink in the distance.

Now, he steps onto the grass, still damp from an earlier autumn rainstorm, and follows the beams shining through the clouds like spotlights. The fingers of the gods, his love had always called them.

A flutter of red catches his eye as he makes his way past the back fence and into the field beyond, and as he looks up, he smiles at his feathery companion. A peace fills him. A sense of calm like he's never felt before, washes over him as the clouds disperse and the sun, low on the horizon, paints the sky in the most brilliant light he's ever seen.

As he takes another breath, this one easier, lighter in his lungs, somehow, he feels a familiar hand in his. Looking down, his eyes meet the clear, deep blue gaze of his young bride, her braid of silky, strawberry blonde locks draped over her shoulder as she smiles up at him, rosy cheeks damp.

He raises her hand to his lips just as the cardinal's mate joins them and the pair fly in excited circles above their heads. His own hand, smooth and young, feels steady and sure. He winks down at his love, making her giggle in the way he's always loved, and together, they walk along into the golden light, fading into it, as the sun sinks down into the water.

ALIENATION

Barbara Lehtiniemi

JAKE SPEAKS: I WAS ALREADY SWINGIN' THE BAT before I was even proper awake. It was their yellin' that woke me. I knew it were no nightmare.

I always knew they'd come back for me. I've watched out for them every day since the time before. They came at last. In my own flipping bedroom, for pete's sake.

But I was ready for 'em. I'd been sleeping with a baseball bat, ya see?

"Come on you scumbags!" I hollered at them. No way I was going to let them take me again.

I couldn't tell how many of them there were. They had lights in the middle of their foreheads and I was blinded, ya see? I couldn't see their ugly faces. Must have been a half dozen of 'em, anyway. Hardly a fair fight, but I kept a'swingin'.

Then I heard a sound like thunder and that was that. When I come to, I heard the sirens a'howlin' and the critters were gone. Just me bleeding on the sheets. But I made it! Them scumbags didn't get Jake-freaking-Woodham this time!

Alberta speaks: He'd been a strange man from day one. I just never realized to what degree. His mother disappeared when he was 14—some say she ran off—and his father was always sour and silent. I guess that's why he was a bit of a loner. No real social skills to speak of. Maybe it skewed his sense of reality a bit too.

I shouldn't have meddled with his mind. Trudie came up with the plan, but I'm the one who did it. We chuckled over the idea when we met for coffee after the book club meeting. I shouldn't have acted on it. I see that now. I see a lot now.

I liked Trudie. She and I just really hit it off. What a revelation to have someone I could talk to about anything. Not just books and stuff, but anything. I hadn't had a real friend for so long.

It started when I mentioned his behaviour to Trudie. He'd given me a bit of a hard time about going out so much. But I enjoy taking classes and meeting people. He's never wanted to go out anywhere unless there'll be a TV on. I hated begging for money to do something just for me.

Until I got Mom's money, I felt I had to stay home. After

that... well, I began to feel alive, getting out a bit again. Again? No, for the first time, really. Finally, my own car and my own money!

I guess I'm like the caged bird that thinks it's got it good until one day it discovers the door left open. I just hadn't noticed how restricted life with him was until I stepped outside the cage. I'd gotten used to his sullen silence over the years. He did his thing and left me to run the house and mind the kids. It worked out, mostly. I settled for routine and security and learned to forget chasing dreams. I'm hardly a special case.

Anyway, I told Trudie I thought he'd been reading my journal. I used to leave it on my sewing table. Not that I'd written anything I cared about him seeing. It's just the idea of it. It's bad manners to go reading other people's diaries. Even if you're married to them.

One day, he mentioned my Aunt Iris. Just out of the blue. He asked if I'm going to call her. We hadn't seen her since Mom's funeral. But I'd just written in my journal not two days before that I wanted to give her a call. Coincidence? Maybe. Seemed unlikely. It sure got me wondering. And then I told Trudie.

Trudie devised the idea of me planting a bit of bait in my journal. Make something up that would provoke him to comment. Then he'd have to admit he read it in my journal. Something outlandish, so he couldn't explain it away.

I'm not sure why I wrote about Crazy Jake. That old coot who says aliens abducted him back in the 70s. Stupid! It seemed so implausible. I'd never met old Jake in all the time

I lived at the farm, even though you could see the roof of his place over the trees on the next concession.

I guess I could have come up with better bait. I just wrote about seeing Jake Woodham at the knitter's group. I mean, really, Crazy Jake a knitter? I never thought of Cal coming up with idiotic ideas. I figured he'd ask me about it. Wouldn't that make more sense? I just wanted to make him own up to snooping. The whole thing descended into insanity.

When I got home from my knitters' group, I expected to find Cal with a game on in the TV room, where he'd usually be. Instead, I found him slumped in his chair at the kitchen table, ashen faced and trembling. I thought he'd had a stroke.

Cal speaks: She said it was all her fault. Sure as hell wasn't mine.

You knew someday this would happen, Cal. You knew it right from the start. It's all well and good to marry a pretty woman but you gotta watch her like a hawk. Yep, you gotta watch her. Daddy learned that the hard way before mama disappeared. Some still say she ran off with some salesman. Let 'em. That was never gonna happen to this guy, no way.

Watching was easy for a while, no doubt about that. A long while. The kids and the cooking and such kept her too busy to think about getting ideas. Always knew exactly where she was—at home. After the kids grew up and moved out, she started getting itchy. Anyone could see that. Had to keep a close eye out.

Then her mother goes and dies and leaves her some

money. Alberta'd never had her own money before. Kept a tight rein on that. Next you know she's out all the time. It started with a bit of shopping and you figured "fine." But then it escalated to classes up at the college. Knew that'd lead to trouble. Puts thoughts into her head.

Next thing you know she's out almost every night of the week. It's too much. Art classes, book club, knitters' guild, whatever. That's how it starts, right?

You've got every right to go through her stuff, Cal. It's your roof she sleeps under. And, bingo! There it was. Didn't even know she kept a diary, until then. Just goes to show how sly she's been, all these years.

She'd tried hard not to leave any clues. But she's not too clever for Cal. Found his name. Nothing else, but it don't take much to figure out when something's going on. You don't put a man's name in your diary unless there's something to it.

She waltzed out the door that night. Anybody'd figure she'd headed to a ron-dee-voo with him and not to some knitters' thing. Anyone would. Knew what had to be done. Why take that shit? Grabbed the gear and got going. It's just one road over, but the ground was frozen so I couldn't see her tire tracks in the lane.

Barely enough light to see by that time of night, well after sunset. Flipped the headlamp on. Door wasn't locked quite tight, so it's no crime to go in and look, right?

Heard noises coming from one bedroom. Moans and the like. Barged through the door screaming bloody murder.

But she wasn't there. That's what made no sense. Just

that maniac hollering and swinging a bat. Wasn't really going to shoot him but it was self defence, right? Wasn't going to shoot anybody. But he's swinging a bat, right? So, yeah, it was self defence. After that there wasn't much to do but go home and wait for her and see what she had to say for herself. Didn't wait long.

After she fessed up to what she'd done, sirens started wailing. Lights already shining through the windows. Well, Cal old boy, you screwed that one up from the word go. Shoulda just waited for her to come home and buried her alongside mama.

DANDELION SEEDS

Ronald Zajac

SLOWING HIS STEPS AS HE NEARED THE underpass, Patrick Morrow felt certain of two things: the sanctity of art, and acid reflux.

The latter he called his "walking impediment"—a burning sensation in the lungs and windpipe, as if he'd run too hard in the cold. It increased at the same rate his inspiration waned. Betraying his lectures at the college about the perils of artificial intelligence, he'd turned to an AI health app for an answer, and its conclusion made sense. His midlife malaise manifested as unwanted acids.

This morning he'd tried, and failed, to paint the sunset he'd photographed at the lake over the weekend. A sublime sunset, he thought, but for reasons unknown the Divine

Light did not bless it. He should have expected the acids to taunt him after that.

No matter. If the Divine Light that turned a sunset into a painting was no longer operative in him, if he was on his way to being superannuated by software, he would at least make himself useful by defending the sanctity of other people's art —especially the work of his students. Stomach acid and bilious rumination would not keep him from the Save the Mural drive. And while Patrick Morrow would be a 'Yes' on the matter of saving art from erasure, on principle and without question, he figured he should still see the work up close.

Speculation in the *Port Fulford Times* had it that visual arts students at the college, unsatisfied at the slow pace of city hall's transition to a Climate-Conscious Community, snuck into the underpass in the early morning hours to paint the mural on the western wall. It would have taken a group of them, and a few nights, to do something so elaborate, while avoiding detection under those underpass spotlights. Patrick hoped to discern, by finally observing the mural up close, which of his students could have been part of this guerilla-art operation. That much he could still do, acid reflux be damned.

City staff wanted to erase the whole thing, "to avoid setting precedents on municipal property," but the mural's defenders organized quickly, with a petition, a Facebook page and "Spare the Seeds" accounts on Instagram and TikTok.

The walking impediment got worse as Patrick slowed down, reviving the cancer fears he thought he'd silenced with his one AI inquiry. Once, more than a decade ago, he sprinted from the downtown core, downhill, to the Riverside Parkway loop, switched on by a foghorn to get a photo of a cargo ship emerging from the mist, an image that turned into one of his best-known paintings. It would hang at the entrance to City Hall, then the college, before ending up in a private gallery in Toronto. That sprint would have been the better part of a kilometre and a half, and his lungs did not burn.

The newspaper photos and Instagram posts did not convey this mural's own Divine Light in its fullness. It was a youthful, activist Light, naïve but purposeful. Years ago it might have impressed him less. A beautiful woman, carefully ambiguous in her ethnicity—she could be Asian, Latina, Indigenous—gently blew dandelion seeds from their stem. They rose above familiar Port Fulford landmarks under a sepia-coloured Blade-Runner sky. The higher seeds metamorphosed, some into doves, but most into words, "Cleanse," "Heal," "Revere" "The" "Earth," all of them radiating beams that pierced through the dystopian smoke to open up patches of glorious blue sky.

Patrick's acid conflagration spread as the woman's eyes and the graceful pattern of the dandelion seeds conjured phantoms of inspirations past, while in his head he narrowed the list of potential culprits among his pupils and prepared a rebuke to the tired cliché that was these dandelion seeds and the mystification of the woman of colour for political ends—no matter how laudable those ends. The bicameral response, marvel and deconstruct at the same time, was how it worked for him—but now the burning in the lungs got too intense for acid reflux and the pain migrated to the upper chest, a bit to the left, a concentrated fire-point, with sweat and nausea and dizziness. The tingling in the fingers of both hands became a loss of feeling. Patrick pulled the phone out of his pocket but the fingers wouldn't close and it fell just as the bang of a passing truck shook the sidewalk; the fire-point heated up to supernova and he heard the scream coming out of his mouth without feeling it in his lungs as he fell back against the mural.

You should have seen it coming, Patrick told himself as he waited to see if this would end with the pain subsiding or with the biggest sunset of all. *You should have seen it coming and you should have realized that losing your flashes of inspiration, and worrying about your divine talents being replaced by AI art, were nothing more that another acid reflux excuse, mistranslated symptoms of the crepuscular despair that comes with being surpassed by your own students, superannuated not by some nebulous technology stealing pictures off the Internet but by kids who sneak out at night with their own ideas about the relevance of art.*

Lily Feng sat yoga-style by the creek, trying to concentrate her thoughts on the one white dandelion touched by the sunlight. Not long ago, this embankment was full of them, white parachutes flying away in the wind—it was probably what inspired those people to paint that mural in the underpass behind her.

Lily started coming here, to think and to cleanse, months before they painted the mural. Now it got harder to concentrate with all the cars slowing down, all the strollers and Instagram selfie-takers. Talk on campus was that some of the visual arts kids painted the mural, sneaking out of the residence at midnight. People were excited. Lily wished she could be excited in just that way. It's hard to join in the excitement sometimes, when the little voices in your head— and the more aggressive voices on campus—keep insisting you don't belong there.

Maybe she didn't.

Lily stared more intently at the dandelion, at the one seed sticking out above the others, wanting to fly off. Mà Ma is a nurse in China. But this is Canada...

"Yeah, right! This is Canada and we don't need more of you here!"

She closed her eyes. Mà Ma and Bà Ba tried to prepare her for the racism, some of it in her face, most of it more subtle. She'd absorb that sort of thing more easily were it not for the melancholy fog that filled up the head-space she needed to concentrate on her studies. Now she wasn't sure if the slipping of her grades caused this dark fog, or if the darkness was always there and it caused her studies to stumble. Mistakes magnified, a fog of guilt that spread across her thoughts. She was letting her parents down.

Lily opened her eyes. The seed shook in the wind, still tethered to the plant. Above and behind her a large truck rumbling into the underpass hit a pothole so hard she could feel the shockwave. She looked beyond the dandelion at the creek, barely moving, almost all dry. This time think of water—

—the scream shatters her thoughts—from above, the underpass—

—she springs up, feels for her phone, runs up the slope unready for the moment, feeling insufficient, the wrong one to be here, though in her bones she knows what that scream is and maybe knowing it so well means she does belong right here...?

An older man leans in pain against the mural wall, his back right beside the beautiful woman blowing dandelion seeds. Lily gets to him, tries to talk to him but he is incoherent. She dials 911, taking a breath to remember all the English: ambulance... Westminster Boulevard underpass... male in his fifties, possible heart attack...

As she takes a second to breathe she recognizes him from the college. There is a defibrillator at the college, but it's too far to run. An art teacher. Maybe he has something to do with this mural? His eyes are closed.

"He's breathing hard, diaphoretic," she tells the dispatcher.

As the dispatcher updates her on the ambulance, Lily tells her she is a nursing student, hears herself say that even as the man's eyes open. "Get him sitting," the dispatcher tells her, though of course she knows that.

"Can you hear me?" she asks. "You are Mister Morrow, yes?"

"You know the patient?" the dispatcher asks.

"I know his name—just a second please."

Lily places both hands on his upper arms, her head bent over awkwardly to the right side to keep the phone to her ear, squeezed to her shoulder. "Come on, Mister Morrow, you need to sit down. Here... slowly now. I'm going to help you sit down... it's going to help."

As he lets her ease him down he asks where his phone is. "Right here. Just a second. Are you able to take aspirin, Mister Morrow?"

"You have aspirin?" the dispatcher asks.

Behind her, a car stops. Onlookers. A question through a car window she can't make out.

"Yes... aspirin," Morrow says.

Lily reaches into her right pants pocket for the small flat container, the pills she takes when the college gets too much and it all turns into a headache. There are three left. She gives him two. "Here, chew on these. It will help. I am giving him two regular aspirins to chew on."

"That's really good of you," the dispatcher tells her. "Most people don't have the aspirin ready. You said you're a nurse?"

"Nursing student."

"Well, good on you. You get an A."

Mister Morrow, sitting on the sidewalk now, is chewing on the aspirin when she finally hears the siren coming from the south, up Westminster toward the underpass. A car-horn blast makes her flinch—some driver angry at the onlookers blocking the way. Traffic starts moving again on the lane right behind her as the ambulance gets closer from the other direction.

"The ambulance is here," she tells both of them.

"Okay, good," the dispatcher answers. "Listen, you did great."

She says "thank you" but is not sure whether the dispatcher has already disconnected. The woman's words echo in Lily's head and she realizes the fog is all blown away.

"Are you still in pain? Are you feeling nauseous?" she asks Morrow.

He lifts his eyes to her. "Um, yes... Yes to both..."

Morrow looks at her in the strangest way; she can't figure out what is going on behind that gaze but it doesn't have anything to do with his pain or his heart attack.

The ambulance stops in the far lane, lights flashing, while another siren grows louder, from the north. Two men and a woman run out of the ambulance. The female paramedic is hefting the defibrillator-monitor while the men run ahead to deal with Mister Morrow.

"I gave him two aspirin just now," Lily tells them. "He's still in pain and feeling nausea. Short of breath, diaphoretic."

"You're a professional, I see," one of the two men says, not looking at her but focusing on Morrow's face.

"I'm... no, I am... a nursing student."

"Did you get him seated like this on the sidewalk?"

"Um, yes, I—"

The man quickly turns to her now, to face her. "Trust me, you're a professional."

Both men help the female paramedic as she sets up the heart monitor, and for a few seconds Lily hears nothing but an incoherent sound-stream as the paramedic's words fill her heart; she is a dandelion seed floating higher than any seed has ever been lifted, and right now she can choose which way the wind blows her, and it will take her straight back to the college where she belongs.

When she snaps back to the sidewalk the police car is north of the underpass, blocking both lanes. A policeman jogs past them until he is far enough south to stop the traffic.

While the men carry on their questioning of Morrow, the woman with the heart monitor decides defibrillation is not needed. She looks at her readout while asking Lily all the usual things: how she found him, what she did, whether she knows him.

"We'll get him to the General and it looks like we caught it on time," she says. "You did good!"

The pain did subside—in his chest, at least, though now Patrick felt a sweaty discomfort everywhere and his back hurt no matter which way he twisted. He must have blacked out, because his awareness left him and came back with this young Asian woman grabbing his arms.

He wanted his phone back—he'd have to call someone at some point. The girl gave him aspirins to chew on—bless her.

He thought he recognized her from the mass of student faces at the college. Maybe the aspirin would stop the back pain, which was getting worse.

So this was not the Big Sunset, Patrick thought. So there's that. But it didn't speak in favour of his painting any more real sunsets. He had been denying to himself, for months now if not years, that he was finished as an artist. Now people in white coats holding clipboards would tell him the severity of his heart attack, laying to rest that other bit of denial about acid reflux. All of this whizzed through his brain-scramble of consciousness, like a siren, while he sat on the pavement and the girl spoke on the phone to the 911 people. Now he'd have to think of this mural as the place where he had a heart attack.

The young woman's voice, asking him if he was still in pain, still nauseous, dispersed these thoughts.

"Um, yes... Yes to both..." he replied. He wanted to explain that the pain moved from his chest to his back, but as he looked up at her she started to glow in that indefinable way and as the ambulance stopped and opened its doors Patrick Morrow knew he had his inspiration back. So the Divine Light had a sense of humour... Was this a near-death thing or did he just have to jam his heart-gears to get its attention now? What remained of that heart resurrected as this young Chinese woman's eyes aged before him in the glow of the Divine Light, took on the experience of generations as she assessed him and kept talking on her phone. Her face, radiating care, concern, competence, imprinted in his mind and he wanted it to stay there, past the hospital and the pain to come, to endure long enough for the canvas. Could he get her to pose for him, later, when he got better? Now Patrick Morrow knew he would survive this thing and paint again, call it "The Face of Healing." He would tell his class that true art happens like *this*, flashes that will never appear to an artificial intelligence that can't feel pain, can't feel fear and the omnipresence of death. Inspiration happens when the accidents of existence collide with frail human organisms and damage them just enough to expel a cry of ecstasy.

He looked up, past the two paramedics trying to talk to him; he wanted to speak to her, but she looked up and away, to something in the distance.

One of the paramedics asked him about his emergency contact. Patrick couldn't decide between the ex he didn't want to lean on, and the daughter he didn't want to alarm.

As the paramedics loaded Mister Morrow into the ambulance he asked Lily what her name was. She told him, and told him she studied nursing at the same college where he taught. Mister Morrow thanked her, for the fourth time. He sounded really excited all of a sudden and said he wanted to get in touch, "after all this."

The paramedic who'd spoken to her on the sidewalk started closing the ambulance door from inside. "We're all good. I mean it—you're a pro. You did everything right."

As the door shut, the woman, in the window of the other door, gave Lily a thumbs-up.

The ambulance pulled away.

Lily felt her own heart slowing down after the adrenaline surge. She turned to the mural, remembering now that the city wanted to erase it. The woman's eyes as she blew at the dandelion seeds called to her with gentle encouragement. She could be Chinese, just like her. Or Chinese-Canadian. Why not? She blew gently at the dandelion and her breath turned the seeds into words and doves that healed the sky. That was her purpose—she belonged here. And though the city wanted to erase her there were all kinds of people who were fighting for her, fighting to keep her here in this underpass because they agreed this is where she belonged.

Lily grabbed her phone again and took a picture of this beautiful woman. Yes, she could get excited about this.

FLIGHT

Liz Torlée

'M WEARING A GREY WIG TO MY BABY DAUGHTER'S funeral so no one will recognize me. Waiting in the shadows of a side street off the main square, I watch the attendant usher the mourners into the church, and wrestle with the better woman who haunts me, the one Richard thought he'd married. *That* woman would be bent over with a sadness that makes her gasp for air. I try to feel it, the kind of grief that robs you of any desire to live. I rip the tag off the hat I bought and lower the veil over my face.

They are all inside now. The square is empty but, wary of a straggler or two, I lean heavily on the cane the way I'd practiced and make my way to the mournful tolling of the tenor bell.

I come from a long line of women who never should have had children. I am the last of them and this will be the last day of my old life.

The church smells of incense and furniture polish. A light breeze drifts through the oriel windows, flattening the flames of the beeswax candles. I hope to blend in with those few old women, bent, shrouded, nameless, who are fixtures in any place of worship, and remember to cross myself with the holy water. I choose a seat behind a stone column near the back. There are more mourners than I expected, but a child's death will always bring them out.

In nomine Patris et filii et Spiritus Sancti ...

They say the water was unusually rough the morning our baby girl was found. Most days, the lake barely stirred itself to spill a few ripples on the beach. But that storm blasted in from the north and churned up the water, making the boats at the jetty bob and bang into each other.

Maybe her body had been wedged under the trees that lean over the bay, almost horizontal. The rough water must have broken her free, a whole summer after she'd gone missing. Two kayakers were trying to make it to shore. They overturned and saw her below them. One of them panicked with the shock and nearly drowned. After they were all brought in, the storm blew itself out, and the lake fell silent again.

Requiem aeternam dona eis, Domine ...

Thelma, from the Residents' Committee has snagged a front row seat. How she would have loved taking charge of all the breaking news, with that somber expression and barely disguised glee. ... *"Did you know the mother's disappeared now? Well, the shame of it. I always said people should be more careful. There's a steep shelf down. A child can easily go under. We sent out a warning with the flyer, but does anybody take any notice?"*

There are flowers everywhere. The arrangement closest to me has a small teddy bear in the middle with a bow at its neck. The bear looks like it's choking, its white beady eyes rolled back.

I search the front row for Richard. There he is, head bowed, narrow shoulders tense. I used to love the way his hair fell just an inch over his collar. I could curl it into my fingers when I pulled him close to kiss me. He has cut it short now.

There's a tight fist of panic in my stomach. Why did I come? What if he recognizes me? I imagine his disbelief and anger as he registers this new deceit. Does he never think of those early, shining, hopeful days when I was all he could ever want, before he realized he'd married the wrong kind of woman, one who grew up with no role models for motherly love. If only I could go to him, try to explain one more time. Maybe that's why I came.

The priest is droning on. Dammit, I won't beg. I'm through begging.

Mommy, Mommy. My daughter's voice was far away. A fly was buzzing around my face. I swatted at it. *Mommy, Mommy!* God, what now? It was so hot that day. My shoulders were burning. I turned over on the lounger. In my half-dream, I reached for the suntan lotion and jammed the pink hat back on her head. *What do you have to do to make them listen?*

A long shadow fell across me. "Sorry to bother you. No peace for the wicked, eh?" I opened one eye. Barney, our neighbour. "This blew up on our deck." He was holding my straw hat and scanning the lake, shielding his eyes. "Looks like we're getting a lovely sunset today."

Sunset? I forced myself awake, sat up, and checked my watch, reaching for the hat. "Thanks, Barney."

"Little one back in the cottage, is she?"

There was a funny taste in my mouth, the one you get when you fall asleep in the day. I looked around. The inflatable white swan with its grinning face was lying on its side at the edge of the water, partly covered in sand. "Yes, yes—" I leaned forward. "She must... she went back for something." Barney did a wave-salute and moved on.

I got up. A plastic bucket. I called her name. A white sandal. Two sandals. I went into the cottage. It was empty and silent; no wet, sandy footprints on the floor. I called her name again, louder this time, and walked down to the water. I was not going to run. Not yet. Surely, any second now, I can flop back on the lounger—*"How many times do I have to tell you?"* I scanned the shoreline and stared across the lake. The lake stared back, a fiery orange bleeding along the horizon. The swan with its manic, frozen grin bobbed against my ankle. My breath stuck in the back of my throat. I grabbed the swan by its neck and stumbled up to the cottage.

Dies irae, dies illa, solvet saeclum ...

I bristle at the Latin. Whose idea was that? Richard was hardly a devoted Catholic. I turn my head from the stony glare of the martyred saints on their pedestals.

Mommy, Mommy. Yellow police tape around our cottage. Amber alert. Hordes of media vans with satellites. The divers were called off after four days. Cottagers went out looking every weekend, and permanent residents got tired of them trawling the shores. My daughter stared at me from lamp posts, shop windows, televisions, and social media sites. Those unblinking brown eyes. Richard wept all the time. I couldn't. I'd been taught not to. *"It's your own fault. You should look where you're going." "You can come out when you stop snivelling. Then we'll see how hungry you are."* Crying made everything worse.

Finally, the recessional, the rummaging for hats, jackets, bags. The casket glides down the aisle to "Ave Maria," flurries of mourners crossing themselves as it passes by. Startled by the lump in my throat, the threat of grief, I watch Richard shuffling behind it. There's a woman with him, that girl from his office. She has her arm around him, almost holding him up. A man I don't know is steadying him on the other side. I step closer to the stone pillar and lean with more exaggeration on the cane. Richard is looking straight ahead, his fine features set in a grimace of pain. As he draws level with me, he glances to the side and pauses for just a heartbeat before turning back and following our baby girl through the high, open doors and into the glare of the afternoon sun.

In the bathroom at the airport. I stare at my real face in the mirror, the one no one will ever love again. My hair is flat from the wig. I dig out my brush and fluff it up, put on the new lipstick I bought, press my lips together and blot them with a tissue. They're calling my flight.

WOLVERINE

Gary Kirchner

'LL START WITH ME RAKING EXTER'S LOUTISH grinning cat-face with my nails. My brother would have been proud of that. "Don't think like a tabby," he would scold me. "Think of the most vicious animal you can. Lioness, tigress, whatever. Become it." I became a wolverine. Is a female wolverine a wolveriness? Who cares. My brother taught me a lot about fighting.

Exter yelped, to my gratification, and before he recovered I bit into his shoulder, quickly, piercing with my sharp teeth. I swatted him again with my other paw and this time caught a piece of his ear. He stepped back, frightened, bloodied, and I glared at him, just daring him to come at me again.

He didn't. I picked up my stolen fish in my mouth and disappeared within the chaotic labyrinth of collapsed buildings and concrete and twisted metal that we called the Beauty.

Somewhere further on I emerged onto what once was a street, although now it was pockmarked with holes and strewn with building detritus. Carcasses of destroyed structures leaned inward like lurching giants. They cast no shadows; with day distinguished from night only by a brightening of the gloom, there wasn't enough light for such things.

Five cats slunk out from behind a huge angular block and confronted me. They were emaciated, sickly. Fur was matted, missing in places. One was covered in sores. I felt no revulsion; one gets accustomed to this. And I felt no sympathy; that feeling had vanished a long time ago.

I recognized them, and they recognized me. They wanted my fish. They wanted me to drop it, drop it and go away. They were scared of me, and with good reason. In their condition, if they'd attacked I would have killed three of them before they overcame me. But they were desperate; they were starving. And starving cats will do anything.

Well, I wasn't about to give up my fish.

So with no warning I leapt to my right and raced into a fissure. I was quick, and they were weak. And nobody knew these passages as well as I did. The five raced after me, but soon three of them gave up. Then another. One continued the chase, the one with the least to lose, the one with the sores. He chased me with the energy of pure desperation.

I stopped suddenly and turned around, dropping the fish

and putting my paw on it.

"Go away, Tika," I hissed.

"Give me half your fish," he answered. His eyes were the colour of blood.

"No."

He lunged at me, and I killed him.

Such was our life. Everything had been scarce since the sky turned dark. Nobody provided for us.

We fought each other.

We formed clans.

We stole when necessary.

I managed better than most of the cats, simply because I was more vicious.

I also had my sister to look after.

My sister. She hadn't been able to cope. Or, rather, her way of coping was blissful abandonment of reality. She'd retreated into her own inner world, and now she lay in the bed she'd made of torn papers and old books, staring at them as if they had meaning, sometimes licking her paws. She never spoke, never did anything to provide for herself. A mental invalid. If I didn't bring her food, she'd starve. I'm not even sure she'd notice if she did.

I kept her hidden. She was no threat to anybody, but in the open she would have been raped. If not by Exter, then by Nemiah or Halyon or a hundred others who lurked in the Beauty. Everyone got raped. Except for me, because you don't mess with a wolverine. But everyone else did. That's just the way it was now. It didn't seem to be a big deal. Some even gave themselves, for food or whatever. I don't judge;

you do what you have to do. Some have families.

No kittens, anywhere. Despite the raping and the giving, there hasn't been a pregnancy here in years. Which leads me to the conclusion that in the not-too-distant future there won't be any cats here at all. It'll just be the Beauty.

But what does that matter to me? I'm a survivor. I provide for myself and my sister. I don't waste energy pondering the future of my species.

It would have mattered to my brother, of course. He was that type. Idealistic. We'd been orphans, we three. He was older; I suppose he was from another litter. He always knew so much more about the world than I did. He took care of us. My sister was normal then, and he would tease us and make us laugh.

I'm a homely cat, not that there's any consequence to that these days. But when I was young I got picked on a lot. I remember one time: six or seven mean cats were there, making fun of me. A particularly large bully cat stepped in front of the others and tried to take something from me. I don't remember what it was, but I remember I tried to keep him from taking it. The sun was shining—there was a sun in the sky back then—and I remember there was a bicycle, shiny and red, with candy-cane handle bars and a little pennant on the left side. Funny how certain details stick in your memory. He must have bit me or hit me or something, because I remember being curled on the ground and crying. And then my brother was there. His face was like something I'd never seen. Furious. Savage. They fought, he and the big cat, and I was scared because the big cat was so huge and mean. But my brother beat him up good. Real good. At the end the big cat was bloody and torn and could barely limp away. Then my brother turned to the other cats, a trickle of blood coming from his mouth. "Anyone else?" he said. The others put their heads down and slunk off.

My brother was the first to try to organize the cats, once the bombs stopped falling.

I was grown up then, but just as terrified of what was happening as that little fraidy-cat. At least I was in better shape than my sister, who had crawled into the shell of her own world. She was useless. But my brother was the opposite. He was always a leader, always one for action. He saw the chaos around us and he understood things, things that had to be done.

He went and stood out in the open, even while smoke still rose from smouldering areas in the Beauty, and called out for cats to join him. He spoke with urgency and with vision. Passionate. Strong. I would hang back, hidden amongst heaps of metal like most of the cats, and watch him. I was so proud.

And many cats joined him. There were fights, of course, fights all over the place, fights every day. Our little surviving society was as chaotic as the Beauty. But my brother was the best fighter. And his fighting prowess only added to the weight of his words; his following grew.

But he kept warning me when we were alone. "It's going to get mean," he said, "because that's the way cats are. Remember what I've told you."

And one day they turned on him. Just like that. He was

there with his group of followers, and suddenly other cats emerged like foul breath from lairs hidden in the confusion of broken concrete. They killed my brother, his followers, his vision.

I arrived just after it had happened. And that's when I became a wolverine.

They say the sky is getting brighter, but I don't see it. It looks as brown and opaque as ever. Maybe it's brighter. Maybe one day there will be a sunrise. Maybe one day there will be a sunset. Truth is, I don't care anymore.

I squeeze through familiar rubble into the austere but cozy cavity I call home, the fish still in my mouth. I drop it on the ground. My sister is there, of course, in her corner with all the books. One is open, and she's holding a pencil as if she's able to write with it.

"No!" I cry, yanking the pencil from her grasp and tossing it away. "You can't hold it! You can't hold things like that! That's not a hand you have! It's a paw!"

MINUTES LOST IN DEATH'S DOUBT & OTHER UNPLANNED SUNSETS

Cheryl Skory Suma

FOR A LONG TIME, I DOUBTED DEATH. WE SPENT decades circling one another before I granted her the undivided attention she so desperately coveted.

Tick, tock, tick, tock. That clock is distracting. Confusing my chain of thought. It's hard to find the beginning, so let's start with the clock.

I'm old enough to recall when clocks hung freely and proud with purpose. Ornamental yet functional, they marked the passage of time for all to see. Today, no one wears a watch anymore, and wall clocks have become scarce. They've faded away, along with video cassette rentals and children sent outside to play unsupervised on the streets until dusk. With all of us focused on our phones, the face of time is no longer an obligatory display in public spaces, it seems. How little we all know. Visible ticking clock or not, death is in the minutes.

I wish I could say my career was planned, but honestly, I fell into advertising. I'd always loved to weave stories, to entertain, but in the end, my greatest gift turned out to be the art of "look here, not there." That is what advertising is all about, the art of illusion. Convincing the audience that their attention, needs, and desires should all be focused somewhere else. The truth is, it's the stuff in the shadows you should be worried about. The things we don't tell you, the things we put in the very, very, tiny print that you never read. We are master magicians. We sell dreams, miracles, unicorns. We sell sunsets.

When I discovered I had cancer, it felt like a poorly woven sales pitch. Another sunset that I could afford to miss. A masquerade, a bad joke that everyone should have seen through. A poorly planned ad campaign that I could walk away from and ignore. Unfortunately for me, it was all too true.

Clunk—the hand moves forward.

I remember when I was little, setting off with my mother to visit my sick aunt. We stood in the middle of the crowded train station while she tried to figure out which track was ours. As my mother fretted, I stared at all the newness, at the strangers passing by. I happily bathed in the excitement of all that hurriedness.

My mother kept worrying aloud about the time, cursing the clock, which caused me to look up to where one hung on the station wall. *How could our delay be the clock's fault,* I wondered?

I couldn't believe how large and beautiful it was; a shining moon suspended high above the crowd. Its brass hands looked too substantial to move on their own. I was pleasantly startled when I heard the ominous clunk of the minute hand lumbering forward, doggedly marking the passage of time. It had managed to etch the lost minute on its face after all. Although just 6, in that instant, I fully appreciated the relentless certainty of its course. The last minute marked, then lost, becoming part of the past. Perhaps the clock was to blame.

Marked, then promptly forgotten. I pulled a juice bottle from my backpack and returned to people-watching. What is the value of time, after all, when you are 6?

For as long as I can remember, my mother was dying. By the time I turned 7, she'd taught me that she might disappear at any moment. By all measures, she was a healthy, vibrant woman, but for my brother and me, she offered another reality. We both recall with painful clarity those moments when Mom's death days would come. My mother dramatically reposed in her bedroom, the curtains shut, lights dimmed, calling us to her bedside. Her feeble, whispered tone implied the end was near as she sternly warned, "Your mother could die any time."

Turns out, she wasn't really in any imminent danger. When I was 13, I developed migraines and discovered first-hand what all my mother's dying had been about. No longer fearful of her demise and angry for the anxiety she'd instilled, I vowed to never fear death again.

I've settled nicely into each stage of life—I've never been one to feel old. Even now, with three adult children (two married, the youngest doing things in reverse by having a child first, with a wedding on the horizon), I still feel young. Right up until my diagnosis, I felt healthy, vibrant, alive. I swam laps almost every day. I tended to my herb garden so I could create gourmet meals with that added gift of freshness. I loved to dance, to host dinner parties for friends and family, and I was always up for another friendly debate, another good conversation, even the occasional new adventure pushed by my children or my risk-seeking partner.

Until this year. Until 58, when my stomach swelled up almost overnight, causing my trim, fit body to finally morph into something more suiting my age, I suppose. The doctor said it was ovarian cancer mixed with two atypical variants. My swollen abdomen was due to a cancerous fluid called ascites. He suggested a procedure to drain the fluid, followed by some chemo, possibly an operation to remove the bulk of the cancer. Then he told me the truth.

My brand of cancer was a fancy-named one that I'd

never heard of before. The kind that drove my doctor to look carefully over my shoulder as he talked. The kind that made him say you should get your affairs in order. The kind that, once named, hangs in the room like a sinking balloon, helium failing, slowly but certainly drifting toward the floor to settle without fanfare in its final resting place.

The minute counting kind.

Suddenly, death and I had become reacquainted with earnestness. I wasn't looking for a new friend, so once I recognized her, death tried to stick to the shadows, preferring to drift in and out of my sightline. We both understood she'd get to me, but only when she was good and ready.

When she'd gathered enough minutes.

Thirty years ago, when I chose to marry, we still carried around video cameras. My husband and I took one on our honeymoon. Hours of footage of us, unabashedly cheerful, playfully documenting our journey for our unknown fans. Enjoying our time in the bubble of new romance.

I've watched those clips, one in particular, over and over. It's from our time in Australia. We'd gone on a long hike, one that first wove several miles down a wrapping staircase strung into the mountainside. Just the steepness of that climb now makes me dizzy, sitting middle-aged and stout on my too-soft couch, amazed at this youthful me, at her bravery and easy smiles displayed on the screen.

I watch as the two adventurers climb down to the valley floor to chatter and tease their way through the valley's lush, tropical path. The young woman in the video is foreign to me, a blissful stranger who does not yet comprehend what the future will hold. She can't possibly be me. I was never that happy, that beautiful, that carefree. I stare at the video, fascinated, wanting to connect with her energy. To feel her certainty. But I can't, as she and I are lost to one another, made strangers by the passage of time. I, swathed in hurts, unexpected experiences, and the gifts of aging and illness until I am hidden from her, and she, unable to envision the future me.

Still, I envy her, even if I doubt she genuinely existed as she presents on screen. Powerful and free of fear, laughing and joking with me from inside the outdated video cassette.

I whisper-think a bargain with death. I don't want to be greedy. I don't need that lost girl's youth, her extra time still ahead, her beauty, or her health. Just let me feel her certainty, her belief that the best is yet to come. Her ignorance of the passage of minutes. Of the clock's clunk.

Let me be, once again, deaf to the clock.

Sometimes, when I'm feeling more brazen, I imagine I could chase death around the room. To force her to flee from me instead of the other way around, even if we could only switch roles for a moment. The two of us running faster and faster as I pursue her in ever closer circles. I chase death until we both collapse, winded, silently agreeing to a temporary truce.

I know this fantasy can't be, for stalkers never stop stalking. They're too committed.

It was as if all of my thoughts and feelings now sat on

little wooden blocks, each one stacked precariously onto the next. A toddler's tower threatening to topple at any moment, to scatter pieces of me until nothing is left but a purposeless mess.

To say the last few months have been difficult would be an understatement. While the chemo did push the cancer back initially, it returned with a vengeance four months after my treatments ended, spreading its web throughout my abdomen and upward toward my lungs. As the various cancer growths began to press on my stomach, intestines, and bowel, my body struggled to digest and pass food.

I knew what came next, and I wanted no part of it. I'd heard the horror stories of cancer patients throwing up their bowel contents—the reality of this kept me up at night more than any discomfort from my condition. In addition, as the cancer advanced, I struggled to breathe. I felt its weight, the cancer pressing on me until I could barely move, until I wondered if I was only still here because of everyone who loved me, everyone who watched and wished and demanded I battle on. What if no one was nearby? Could I cease to exist without their watchful eyes to pull me forward?

In my youth, I was a competitive swimmer at the national level, destined for the Olympics. Until I met my husband. Until my practices were derailed, my dreams fell to the wayside, and my path was altered. I don't regret it. My children are my everything, and they would not exist if I hadn't chosen their father over my teenage dreams.

Still, my youth has flared up in the strangest ways these

last few days, haunting me. Not with its forward dreams—with its struggle to embrace the next minute. I well recall those odd moments after a big race or a long training session when I just wanted to rest in the water's embrace. That feeling of letting myself sink, of letting go of my survival instincts and allowing my body to descend to the bottom of the pool. That moment just before my body started to struggle against me, its instinct to fight against the water's weight overwhelming my desire to lay there permanently.

In my now, my body continues to want me to fight for that next breath, but some part of me just wants to rest, to descend into the water's warm cocoon.

It took some time, but eventually, I came to understand that I'd been consumed with the clock and death's dance for too long. I'd imagined every possible way we'd become one. So many wasted minutes lost along with death's doubt. This morning, as I watched the sunrise, I realized that it was time for us to come to an understanding. Unlike the movies, clarity did not arise from a magical, life-changing moment. It just arrived.

Tick, tock, goes the clock.

There was a power in that last minute. I realized that I could continue to wait for my stalker to grow tired of me and end it, or I could act. There was a way to restore doubt—by accepting each new minute, by holding them close before death had a chance to collect them. By searching out possible joy, however transient. By choosing my own last sunset.

My decision made, I called my palliative care physician,

explaining my wishes. It took a few weeks to sort out, lots of documents to sign, and conversations to be had, but in the end, I was able to pick my own happy ending. My family and I had a lovely celebration of life that went on for three days; everyone I loved gathered in one place, sharing food and stories and love. When the doctor came on the final day to administer MAID, I was ready. Going out on my own terms —not in fear, not in pain, and without doubt.

The time had come to not just acknowledge death as she lurked in the shadows but, instead, to shine a light in her direction. Until she was forced to raise her arm to shield her eyes. Until she felt this last minute with me, rather than just following me around to collect it. After controlling the when and how of my own goodbyes, my final act was to forgive and forget death. I was at peace. I would leave her to doubt.

The time had come to let death understand that this current minute, this last sunset, was mine and wasn't up for the taking.

LUCID OBSERVER

Chris J. Meyer

I T WAS THURSDAY NIGHT AND ALEX HAD ARRIVED at the Dream Forecasting Institute for his weekly appointment. He always looked forward to this evening as a brief escape from the demands of his life. It was a time to unplug and enjoy the small luxuries of a personalized sleeping chamber; a familiar space with plush furniture, subdued lighting, and warm hues overlaid with aromas of citrus and spice. Plus, he felt a sense of purpose contributing to the Institute's goal of exploring the unconscious mind for clues about the future.

Alex took a seat on the side of the bed. Without looking, he picked up the wireless neural relay from its usual spot on the nightstand. He positioned it against the subdermal ports on the back of his neck and it snapped magnetically into place. Alex closed his eyes and breathed deeply as he waited for the Interpretation Technician.

The Tech entered Alex's chamber a few minutes later. She was tall and slender, dressed in a one-piece beige uniform, with her hair pulled back tightly; a clinical professional. Her persona was graceful but direct, calm but exacting, and her eyes deep and mesmerizing.

"Good evening, Alex. Anything to report before we begin?"

"Yeah, there's this recurring dream I've been having that I'd like analyzed. I think there's some troubling details in it that you should look into."

"Very well. Shall I initiate?"

"Yep."

She revealed a syringe, pre-filled with a cocktail of mild sedatives and synthetic neurotransmitters that redirected all sensory signals to the neural relay. Alex had consented to participate in the Institute's lucid observer framework, which had the provocative ability to transmit clear visual and auditory details, including internal thoughts, to a confidential interpreter. The Tech placed a comforting hand on Alex's shoulder before applying the syringe to an insertion port on the relay. Once the solution was fully injected, she discarded the syringe, and then helped him lay down.

"I hope you have a restful sleep."

"Goodnight. I... I..." The sedatives worked quickly, as expected.

The Tech exited Alex's room and walked around the corner, along a short corridor, to a central observation hub. She sat in the centre of the hub surrounded by a long-curved window that contained panes of one-way glass. This allowed her to discreetly examine the sleeping subjects in three separate chambers. Above the window of each chamber was a television screen. When she turned on the screens, they all filled with waving amorphous projections and irregular flecks of light. Such undefined neural imagery was typical at the outset of each session. Suddenly, Alex's projection began resolving and taking shape. The Tech placed an audio receiver in her left ear and began a focused observation.

"What'd ya mean there's no space for me?" … "You're taking that loser! Come on man. We both know that I'm more valuable to have on board than that parasite." … "Okay, how much you want? There's always a price!" … "Hello?" … "Hello?" … "Asshole!"

The audacity to hang up on me in the middle of a negotiation! My rage takes hold as I hysterically punch the wall and swat all the useless trinkets off the mantle. It has been a hectic week, culminating in this explosive day. The lack of sleep is getting to me. How long have I been awake?

All the 24-hour news channels have beat the pulp out of this apocalyptic event. The screen on my right has that shit-for-brains conspiracy theorist ranting again: "Look, the world is not ending! Honestly, when was the last time these so-called planetary experts spent time here on Earth? The weather is beautiful. Sure it's hot, but that's why God created air conditioning. If you ask me, I like not having to worry about hurricanes anymore! Listen folks, go on with your life, there's nothing to worry about here."

The screen in front of me has a panel of concerned scientists providing way too much information: "Since time immemorial we have measured reductions in the speed of Earth's rotation, but these occurred at infinitesimally small increments. However, the rotation has rapidly decelerated with the migration of the red giant Arcturus into our solar system. In addition, Earth's orbit around the Sun began to wobble and decelerate with Arcturus' introduction. For at least the last 5000 years, Arcturus has been lumbering toward Earth, profoundly exerting its gravitational pull, placing us in the centre of a cosmic tug-of-war between the red giant and the Sun. Approximately seven days ago, our planet stopped rotating and its orbital trajectory shifted toward Arcturus. We are officially tidal-locked, with most of Earth's surfaces being constantly illuminated and pummelled with radiation."

The screen on my left has that soft-spoken guru who alternates between affirming phrases and deep breaths: "The end is imminent ... Be with your loved ones ... Reflect on the good times ... You are strong ... Your energy will go on ..."

I dismiss all the screens, wishing they were physical objects that could be smashed.

"Sir? Sir? Alexander?" It's my assistant, Soleil. While it feels like everyone has abandoned me, including all my sycophant employees, Soleil has been steadfast through the pandemonium. I'm always in awe of her calmness, even though I've been unreasonably demanding of her. It's surprising she has tolerated me over these last few years, but I did pay a small fortune for her. I recall the pitch: AI-designed neural networking, best in class polymeric materials, privacy at its core, tireless, life-like, on and on. She absolutely resembles a human. Fools just about everyone who meets her. And the sex... mmm.

"Alexander, are you okay? Do you need my assistance?"

"Well, if you can get me a ride off this searing planet, I'd be forever grateful."

"All remaining shuttles scheduled to depart Earth are at full capacity. Perhaps it is prudent to consider relocating to one of the subterranean bunkers."

"And live among the stench and filth? I'd rather be barbecued up here!"

"I am picking up some radio communications of colonies forming in a meridional twilight zone, approximately 1500 kilometres northeast of us."

"I cannot be seen with those lunatic nomads. If the radiation doesn't kill them, their stupidity will! Listen, I need to get on a shuttle. Do whatever it takes, no matter how unsavoury."

The chances of boarding one of those shuttles is unlikely, perhaps impossible. But if there's a way, Soleil will find it.

I raise the opaque protective sashes from my office windows. For the last week the Sun has been stationary, a watchful eye hovering above the western horizon, creating a permanent late afternoon glow across the city. It's picturesque; a literal snapshot in time. It's an image of a perfect day; a day without end.

But I've come to realize that the important thing about wonderful moments is their rarity and transience. It makes them desirable and elicits genuine happiness. A day without end has all these traits, but only for the first 48 hours or so. Now there is no relief from an ever-present heat and light source. Now the life around me is withered, parched, extinguished.

Damn, I'm starting to think like that guru. I retract the window sashes and sit at my desk. Just need to rest my eyes for a few minutes.

Alex's screen went momentarily blank. The Tech noted his normal vital signs before resuming her observation.

"Sir? Alexander?" I'm rustled awake by Soleil's gentle massaging of my shoulders. "Wha... what time is it?"

"17:30. You were sleeping for—"

"Yes, yes I know, too long! Okay, do you have anything for me?"

"I reviewed the passenger manifest for the final exit shuttle. Many of the registrants are government officials, military, some who you have had financial dealings with."

"Yes, and...?"

"Dealings that overwhelmingly favoured you. Those individuals are not likely to be amenable to your current plight."

"Ah, we could dig up so much shit on any one of those weak, two-faced pricks."

"Yes, but doing so will not secure you a seat."

"Okay, so we take extreme measures. Maybe one of them suddenly falls deathly ill, yeah?"

"No. You need to convincingly earn your seat, and I have identified a way."

"Go on then!"

"Two days ago, a lottery was held for one seat aboard the shuttle. The lottery was exclusive to individuals under the age of 21. That seat was won by a 14-year-old girl named Athena Pallas."

"Perfect! So, I'll convince this kid to cough up her seat to me. Should be a pushover."

"Well sir—"

"Ha, let's offer her half? No, maybe start at one third of my assets and see where she caves. I'll make her think she's won a mega lottery! Soleil, prep a spec sheet for me on this little brat."

"Yes, Alexander."

"And what time does the shuttle leave?"

"Departure is set for 21:00."

"Shit, we need to get down there! Let's take an air taxi. You can give me her details on the way."

As I gather my essential belongings in a small case, I'm abruptly numbed by existential dread. Will I have a legacy if I can't get on that shuttle? Does my unparalleled success matter if I can't find a worthy successor for my business empire? There are no opportunities to be extracted from this global catastrophe; both time and progress have stopped. There's no longer a place for me or my legacy on Earth. I need to get on that shuttle!

The Tech's curiosity got the better of her and she neglected to monitor the other two sleeping subjects. Fortunately for her, they continued projecting amorphous nonsense. She drew her focus back to Alex.

We've arrived at the shuttle station, and fortunately boarding has not yet begun. Before exiting the air taxi, I take a moment to adjust my protective anti-radiation suit and assess the hectic scene on the launch deck: hordes of people swarming around 2000 lucky passengers, all separating me from the shuttle, a colossal life support vessel that is my last semblance of hope.

"Soleil, where's the girl?"

"Athena is near the end of the passenger queue."

"Okay, when we find her, start by introducing me, but make it quick. Let's go!"

"Alexander. Before we exit, I recommend you trigger my memory transfer protocol. Once we secure your place in the queue, we may lose contact. Therefore, I need to be ready to quickly transfer my neural network to your remote controller."

"Ah, brilliant." I caress Soleil's impeccable face. "I will miss this, but at least I can keep your mind."

I leave my left hand on her cheek, take her left palm and place my right thumb in it, then stare into her deep eyes.

"Admin account. Authorization: root user Alexander. Protocol: memory transfer."

"Hello Alexander. Triggering this protocol may have undesirable or unintended effects. Do you understand?"

"Yes."

"Are you sure you want to trigger a memory transfer?"

"Yes."

"The trigger is initiated. It will remain active for 60 minutes."

I kiss Soleil's lips, release my hands, and her consciousness returns.

"Hello Alexander."

"Let's go!"

I step out of the taxi and am struck by a wall of sound. The voices of thousands are overwhelmed by a public address system. "For the survival of humanity, we must migrate toward exoplanet candidates that could support life. Our species are innate explorers, and we have delayed our travel beyond the comfort of our solar system for far too long. Now we are left with no other choice than to rebuild our civilizations elsewhere in the galaxy."

Soleil navigates a path through the crowd at a frustratingly slow pace. She has no difficulty convincing folks to step aside, but there are hundreds to penetrate. I follow her with my head down, being jostled back-and-forth as we trundle forward. The mob's voices have merged into a throbbing groan of desperation, and the stale air among them is suffocating.

Finally, we reach a uniformed border of stern-faced security guards who are shielding the passengers. Soleil approaches one of the guards. After a brief discussion, he steps aside and nods for us to pass. Now we are in a buffer zone that is occupied by what appear to be close supporters of the passengers. There is a low fence that separates us from the rarefied group who are standing in sinuous rows under a long, curved awning that provides some relief from the scorching radiation.

Soleil spots the girl and easily draws her attention. "Hello, Athena? Athena Pallas?"

"Hi, yes, I'm Athena!" She's basking in the glow of the spotlight: the golden child, the saviour of humankind.

"Well, let me start by congratulating you. You must be delighted to play a direct role in the establishment of our new colonies. My name is Soleil. I am an artificially intelligent executive assistant."

"Oh, cool!"

"Yes. But allow me to introduce an admirer of yours, and perhaps a key patron of your future. He is a—"

Enough bluster, we're running out of time! I step ahead of Soleil and launch in.

"Ms. Pallas, hello! What a pleasure it is to meet the star-studded lottery winner. Such a beautiful and charming young woman you are. But can I let you in on a little secret? Or what I've come to know as the big deception!"

"Pardon, sir? A deception?"

"Absolutely. Trust me when I say that this information comes direct from that sleazy roach standing up there." I point toward the shuttle at the President who is greeting all the passengers as they board.

"You and the President will be the last to board. He will

embrace you and make some fantastic sounding promises. Then once on that shuttle, you are his property, his toy. You know why you're being called 'the future of humanity' right? You'll be his baby-making machine!"

Too harsh? Nah, there's no time for subtlety now. As I continue describing the horrors of the shuttle to the girl, I notice that Soleil is communicating with that security guard again. Why isn't she by my side?

"Listen, Athena. I want to help you. I'm willing to relieve you of this burden. I'll take your place on the shuttle, and in exchange I'll give you... oh I don't know... let's say... an even one third of my wealth. That's a generational gift! You can stay here with your family, live in the finest underground estates, and have all your needs met. This is a dream opportunity! What do ya think?" I show her my mobile device with details of the transaction.

"Oh... wow. I think I need to... uh... yeah I should talk with my dad, and—"

"Well, this line is moving and there's no time for further discussion. If you just authorize the contract here, I'll initiate the transfer of funds. Okay?"

Before I can close the deal, the guard seizes me from behind. "What... hey, get off me. What's this about?"

"Sir, I'm taking you into custody."

"Excuse me?"

"You're a safety threat to these passengers. Come with me!"

"No, no! That's false! There's no evidence... wait... Soleil... Soleil help!"

As I'm being pulled away, I'm stunned to see Soleil removing the neural network chip from the back of her neck and inserting it into my remote controller. She calmly hands the loaded controller to Athena, then her body collapses.

What has Soleil done? Was she manipulating me this whole time? For her own escape?

I'm escorted to an outdoor holding cell, where I sit defeated and ponder the thread of events, the multiple possibilities, and my ultimate downfall; deserted by everyone and blindsided by the one entity I trusted above all.

I watch as the shuttle lifts off and exits the atmosphere. The security guard releases me from the cell and guides me to an area to collect my belongings. Soleil's body is lying there, a shell of her former self, with a repeating phrase emanating from her mouth, "Please insert neural chip to activate."

"Hey buddy, how 'bout a drink?" The guard slips a steel flask from his breast pocket and offers it to me.

I take a long pull, then exhale the volatile vapours, "What did she offer you?"

"Does it matter now?"

"Hm..." I glance at the guard's face and notice his eyes... they're so much like Soleil's...

Is he...?

I laugh, shake my head, and take one more quaff from the flask before tossing it back to the guard. Then I strip off my protective suit and walk alone toward that damned picturesque sunset.

The Tech removed her earbud, stood up, and raced to Alex's chamber. Inside, she retrieved a new syringe and filled it from a vial labelled Erasure. Following the injection, Alex slowly regained consciousness.

"Oh, hey... good morning."

"Good morning, Alex. How are you feeling?"

After casually yawning and sitting up, Alex continued, "Great! Another perfect sleep. Hm... so how about my dreams? Anything noteworthy?"

"Well, there were a few short bursts of activity. But the content was consistent with your past projections. Another summary of your week. Hence, nothing of concern."

"Huh," he rubbed the back of his neck in response to an unusual tingling sensation around the neural relay. "So...do you think it's still necessary for me to come here? I mean...it seems like I'm wasting your time since I'm not contributing—"

Shaking her head, the Tech interrupted, "Oh Alex, on the contrary. Each session helps us to further understand the typical dream-state. Myself and everyone at the Institute truly appreciate your participation."

"Ah, well... I guess that's good. Same time next week?"

"Indeed. May I?" She gestured with open hands indicating her intent to detach the relay from his neck.

As she reached back, Alex gazed into her glimmering eyes, and he was rendered unconscious. He came to shortly thereafter, feeling serene and unburdened. He smiled, rose, and left the chamber.

WHEN BRITNEY SPEARS COMES ON THE RADIO

Anne Baldo

"I KNOW WEST," MIKE SAYS. HE WAS ONE OF the baseball players that had come into the bar an hour ago. When I saw him looking over at us, smiling, I smiled back; before long he'd made his way to our table. "He's kind of like, a party guy, you know what I mean?"

"I don't really know what you mean," I say. We are on the patio, a view of twilight traffic on Tecumseh Road, the batting cages at the end of the parking lot. Nobody plays there anymore. The fence around gone wild with weedy vines; dandelions shine up through the fractured asphalt, and for a moment, when the sunset hits our eyes, we can no longer see anything but gold light. Across the parking lot is an expensive furniture store that sells statues of glittery leopards, giant sequinned throw pillows, Italian sofas in teal leather. Next to that, an adult video store whose windows seem perpetually broken, covered in cardboard; the mannequins stand, peering out where the cracked glass remains, listless in lingerie unchanged since the 80s—high-cut satiny underwear, black lace bodysuits, crimpy wigs, and purple eyeshadow.

"I think you do," he says. "Come on. Why? How do you know West?"

But I don't want to say how I know him. How we go out to dinner at Montana's where he won't order carbs and re-minds me not to either, splitting the bill fifty-fifty no matter what we get, and always hits on the waitress then doesn't call for two weeks. So I don't say anything at all.

It's better to forget boys if you can, and just go out with your friends. It's always me and Amy and Claire, in pleated miniskirts, kitten heels, sticky lip gloss that's supposed to taste like watermelon or cherries, or spangled with Jessica Simpson's Dessert beauty products, the ones you ice yourself like cake with. We download Ludacris on Limewire, and in the car, when Britney Spears comes on the radio, we turn the volume way up and sing the lyrics with her. We buy glossy magazines that cash in on her pain, inspect her workout routines, her body at the beach. They interview doctors who estimate her weight like *The Price Is Right* contestants speculating on the cost of a flat-screen TV. Snapshots highlight cellulite, add helpful arrows to point out perceived flaws, and they say she is out of control.

Next to me, Claire raises her eyebrows, tweezed to thin arches, and peels a limp nacho off her plate. At the other end of the table Amy reaches into her sequinned clutch, flips open her phone; Trevor has been calling and calling all night, even though they are supposed to be broken up, but she hasn't changed her ringtone for him, Mariah Carey's "We Belong Together," which is their song, so they'll get back together.

It had been an unlucky day. On the way home from Taco Bell that afternoon, we hit a pothole just before Pillette and the chunk of concrete that dislodged itself from the road crushed my parents' minivan's exhaust pipe. Now, just past dusk, it seemed the unluckiness of the day had mutated into an ominous, restless energy.

We'd spent the day together; after Taco Bell but before the bar, we had gone back to our old high school to pick up our yearbooks.

I'll wait in the parking lot, I said. That summer after high school it's Amy, Claire, and me and we do everything together. We swear we will be each other's bridesmaids. We will get matching tattoos. The three of us will travel the world and always tell each other everything. In real life it turns out we do none of these things. We will not even go to Claire's wedding, and Amy will leave town without telling us. I will see her one day on the sidewalk and for a long moment she won't recognize me before finally she says *oh, Natalie, it's you.*

Amy grabbed my wrist. *Don't you want to get our yearbooks?*

No, I said. *I have three other books filled with the same people.*

It feels like I can't understand anything at all, not just the yearbooks. Like why we acknowledge all the double standards we lived with as girls, but don't do anything about them, or maybe we just couldn't, sometimes. Or the way I know something's wrong with me because anytime I get a chance for something good I just want to ruin it, but I don't know why. Or trying to understand how after spending all year hanging out with Asher, who I'd known since grade school, partnering on history class projects and watching UFO documentaries at his place on the weekends, at the end of the year he'd asked Stacey to go to prom with him, instead, and then messaged me on MSN a week later: *hey.*

Hey.

Alright then, hey, he typed back, as if I'd offered up the wrong response, and I still wonder what it was that I was supposed to say. *Hey anyway.*

"This humidity is wrecking my hair," Claire says in the washroom. Crowded in Amy's bedroom two hours earlier, we took turns flat-ironing each other's hair. Claire in a cargo miniskirt, minty green polo, while I wear a pleated denim skirt, kitten heels, lace-trimmed cami.

"Did you tell your parents yet about the van?" Claire asks. She gives up on her hair, leans into the mirror, fixes her lip gloss. By her side in the reflection, I stare hard, trying to see if lying across the picnic table in my parents' backyard all afternoon yesterday has given me a tan.

You're so pale, West said, running his fingers down my bare arm the last time we were in his basement. Cold downstairs and I tried not to shiver in capri jeans and halter top. *You need to start tanning.*

Alright, I said. *I'll go.*

And when you do, you can use one of those stickers, you know, a little heart or they've got the Playboy Bunny, on your hip or something. And then show me.

"Not yet."

"Natalie," she says. "You have to tell them what happened. What are you waiting for?"

Claire is right; she usually is. She is like our Ann Landers of the new millennium, all advice and etiquette. Like never wearing white eyeshadow, or how you don't want thick eyebrows so we tweeze them, but if you stripped them too thin, that was trashy, a fine line, and that I am not supposed to talk to Asher ever again or even think about him, and the last one is probably true. But we hadn't even talked all summer until last week when we ran into each other here at the bar by the pool tables.

Natalie, Asher said, blue pool cue chalk on his fingers, his gaze fixed on the cleavage I'd built like an architect, taking my best push-up bra from La Senza and then stuffing it with the padding from two other bras. At first I thought I'd liked it, the way he looked at me, and then I'd felt a surge of inexplicable anger. *I didn't think you were like this.*

Like what? I asked, but he didn't answer.

Claire says, "You're going to be good tonight, right, Natalie?"

I nod.

"You have to have higher standards, okay?"

Last winter Claire used to tell me my clothes were wrong; *skirts like that are for girls with perfect thighs*, she said, in the dressing rooms at Winners. *Maybe you shouldn't show your arms.* Now, a year later, she jabs at my bare shoulder. *Natalie, this is gross. Boys don't even like bones.*

Claire grabs my hand, pulls me through the crowd on the way back to our patio table. "I'm just so glad you don't talk to Asher anymore, he is so weird," she says, as if she can read my mind: after all these years we were blood sisters sharing a wavelength. "Remember that time we went over and we had to watch that boring documentary all night?"

"No."

"That statue they found at the bottom of the sea, like, who cares."

"Oh, you mean the unsolved mysteries of the Artemision Bronze?"

Claire snorts. "Do you think I was actually paying attention?"

Amy is still on the phone when we get back, her back bent to us as she tries to hear Trevor through the racket around us: loud clack of pool balls skipping over warped green felt, glass bottles breaking, the rising wave of noise as "Don't Stop Believin'" comes on.

"Do you think Trevor is going to come here?"

Claire rolls her eyes. "Nat, he always does."

Mike is waiting at our table. Claire has been ignoring him, but he seems nice. He has dark eyes, and hockey hair,

Amy calls it, the kind of hair you'd see on a guy in an American Eagle ad, modelling a half-unbuttoned, preppy flannel. "So, did you want to dance? Unless you're waiting for West to show up or something."

"No," I say, tripping when I get up; he holds his arm steady as I clutch it for balance. "Let's go."

Amy snaps her phone shut. "Trevor's on his way," she says. "He'll be here in a half hour. He says he can give us a ride home."

"Good," Claire says. "Then we won't have to pay for a cab."

Mike says, "We're just going to go dance."

Amy's gaze is on the parking lot already, the lights of the furniture store like broken gold over the wrecked pavement. "Alright," she says. "We'll find you."

It was only two months ago I met West here: on the dance floor with Amy, AC/DC shrieking "You Shook Me All Night Long." I noticed him there, at the start of the song, West with his breezy smile, and when the song was over he was there, a drink in his hand, vodka water. *I've been watching you*, he said, reaching for me. He picked me up in his arms, swung me around.

Watching me and my friends?

Only you.

Tonight I let Mike lead me to the dance floor, breathing relief as another drink sets my sprinting mind on steady autopilot, even as I wish I knew another way to feel this way, numb and at peace. Because really I wasn't this girl I pretended to be. I was the girl who spent seventy dollars on a

Simon and Garfunkel compilation set. I was the girl who stayed home Friday night reading *Cryptozoology A to Z: The Encyclopedia of Loch Monsters, Sasquatch, Chupacabras, and Other Authentic Mysteries of Nature*. The girl who was so nervous she faked stomach aches to get out of talking in front of the class. But nobody had liked that girl, really. Nobody even seemed to know that girl was alive. And this person I had become—laughing off everything in a halter top and denim skirt and silver eyeshadow—seemed to finally be a part of the world. People noticed her. *She seems so shallow*, I overheard Claire's friend Heather say last week when we went out. *I didn't think she was like that in high school. Wasn't she kind of a big nerd?* Just tell me who you want me to be, I wanted to say. *Just let me know who I can finally become so that no one will say anything at all.* I felt that for girls, the world was a carnival game, rigged so that we were doomed to lose, no matter how we played.

Don't think about West. I have to remind myself, especially when Mike laughs, the way he closes his eyes, leans his head back, reminding me of West. "Sugar" is playing, and then "Sweet Home Alabama." The music here, a mix of old country, new rap. Mike presses against me, moves with me, close enough to breathe in his drugstore cologne, minty chill of gum, draft beer's yeasty sweetness. He says, *you could come home with me*, and I say *I can't, no*, because it was where I always draw the line: and still Claire had sat me down in her bedroom she shared with her sister, where there is no privacy really because Claire replaced her door with crystal bead curtains, which look super pretty, but I wondered where she changed her clothes. Maybe in the corner, or always in the bathroom. She sat in the desk chair in front of the computer and so I had to sit on the bunk bed, a little hunched over, while Claire swivelled thoughtfully in front of a screensaver of 3D pipes that build and build themselves, endless and neon and tells me I need to be better, to stop acting so trashy, how it's not cute to be easy, how no one really wants that.

Okay, I said, and then I promised to be good. Because Claire was my best friend. We shared eyeshadow palettes in purple, blue, silver. Hoop earrings and furry sweaters, mood rings and tube tops. Claire's voice, a critical constant in my head, my best friend, my conscience. Back then I used to get so angry at Claire and I'd keep it all inside. But I'm not angry anymore. We grew up being taught there was a strict system, and sparse mercy. You could be a girl who saved herself, or the girl who gave it up. And once you did the latter, there was no going back. Weekly, the tabloids reminded us, covers plastered with Britney, our fallen angel, our exiled princess, only a joke now.

But when West was around and he smiled at Claire—his teeth blazingly white, sunlight on snow—I could see that he had her approval, and that I finally had hers too. West, who wasn't *weird*, who was so beautiful. Who looked like the kind of boy you'd be irrational not to love. That he would be interested in someone like me—who could believe my luck? I saw that in her face too.

Maybe I should just go home. Come clean about the damaged van, wash my face, go to bed with a book. We are

18 and we are not even supposed to be here. Or maybe find a payphone, call Asher: tell him it was alright, that I hadn't wanted to go to prom anyway, with him or anyone. Say we could still be friends. I could be friends with Stacy, even. Why can't we still sit in your basement, watch documentaries about national parks and Greek statues and beekeeping? *I should call sometime*, he'd said, *only I forget.*

It's alright, I'd tell him. *I will wait for you, but in the arms of other men.*

When the song ends we stumble off the dance floor, breathing heavy, and Mike tells me he'll get a pitcher of beer, meet me back at the table, maybe I can give him my number and he'll call me tomorrow—

"Alright," I say. But even as he leans down to kiss me, I know that I'm just lying. Because there he is, sitting at a table, staring at the baseball game on TV. West. I walk by and he sees me, standing up, smiling, mouths *come here*, and I do, let him take my hand, pull me in close, hoping he'll feel my hipbones up against him, and that it will hurt a little. Hoping even in the dark he can see my tan but not where the scruff of Mike's beard has scraped my face and neck raw.

"You're drunk tonight, aren't you?" West says.

"No," I say, keeping one hand on the edge of the table. And then he laughs that way I like, leaning back, eyes closed.

Last time West called me, he said, his voice low, *Natalie, tell me something.* And all I could think of was that sunken statue, the Artemision Bronze, so I started talking about that. A mystery statue, found in 1926 off a cape in northern Greece. The question was, who was this statue, really? Some believed it was Poseidon. After all, it had been found in the sea. But had it been placed there, or was it merely underwater because of an unfortunate shipwreck? The statue's hands had once held something, but what? If it was a thunderbolt, then it would be Zeus, but then again the hands could have also held a trident, as Poseidon would have... scholars were looking for clues in painted vases, in coins, and West said, *do you really care about this stuff?*

Yeah, it's interesting—

Natalie, you're so cute.

"You *are* drunk," he says. "I know it. You're a liar. You're still cute though."

I think about how Mike is maybe back at our table, waiting; I think about what I once believed I felt for Asher and now how quickly it was evaporating, as if it never existed; like water that's reached its boiling point disappearing into steam. All the good things that I only ruined and how Trevor would be here soon, no matter what, how the night was almost over and I'd be in the backseat of his car, by Claire's side, while Amy and Trevor argued in the front seat all the way home. But right now West's hand is on my neck, up under my tattoo choker, fingers in my hair which like Claire's, despite our efforts, is wrecked in the summer heat and sticky with our lipgloss, our sweat mixing with our Candie's perfume, floral and peachy. I want him to say what he said before, I want him to say *only you* and for us to both believe it. A moth charmed by a flame is doomed but incandescent, and that last moment before burning must feel just like love.

ABOUT THE AUTHORS

Anne Baldo's (pg. 77) writing has previously appeared in *PRISM, Pulp Literature, Riddle Fence, Carousel, Stanchion, Qwerty*, and the anthology *Wayward & Upward*. Her collection of short fiction, *Morse Code For Romantics*, was recently published by Porcupine's Quill.

Gary Kirchner (pg. 45) holds a Master's degree in sports biomechanics. He played and coached football at McGill for three decades, and taught physics at the college and high school levels during the same period. He is a competitive cross-country skier and a somewhat less competitive curler. His flute-playing is earnest, if not skillful. Gary is the author of the dystopian fiction *Cromby's Axiom* as well as the recently published football trilogy *In the Shadow of the Goalposts*. His first published short story was in *Blank Spaces* magazine.

Barbara Lehtiniemi (pg. 15) primarily resides in the fiction world inside her head and occasionally allows that to spill over to the page. She has published many pieces of non-fiction in several publications including *The Voice* magazine, *The Review* newspaper, *Chicken Soup for the Soul*, and *Maclean's*. She was a finalist in the 2021 *Blank Spaces* Fiction Anthology contest and her story "On Edge" appears in the resulting *The Things We Leave Behind* anthology by Chicken House Press. Barbara has a fondness for travel, used bookstores, and everyday absurdities. She lives on a windswept rural road in North Glengarry, Ontario.

Chris J. Meyer (pg. 63) is a burgeoning creative writer. There was a time in his life when writing scientific articles was common. In fact, he has published several technical pieces in journals with such titles as *Annals of Botany* and *Journal of Experimental Botany*. Although Chris has left that part of his life behind, he maintains a love for plants and science, which is good because he spends most of his time teaching botany to keen undergrads at the University of Guelph. He lives in Guelph with his wife, three conures, and too many houseplants.

Cheryl Skory Suma's (pg. 53) fiction, creative nonfiction, poetry, and photography have appeared in US, UK, and Canadian publications, including *Barren Magazine, Aesthetica Creative Writing Award Anthology, National Flash Fiction, Exposition Review, FatalFlaw Literary Magazine, Longridge Review, SFWP, SugarSugarSalt, Stanchion Zine, the Anthology of the International Amy Macrae Award for Memoir, WestWord, Reckon Review, Pulp Literature, Sonora Review, Blank Spaces* Magazine, and many others. A multi-Pushcart nominee, her work placed in forty-nine competitions since 2019. Cheryl has a MHSc Speech-Language Pathology, HBSc Psychology. Post publication, she joined the team at Barren Magazine as Flash CNF Contributing Editor. You can find her on Twitter/X & BlueSkySocial @cherylskorysuma.

Liz Torlée (pg. 37) claims her ideas are usually sparked by casual conversations with friends, stray remarks that won't leave her head, demanding to be turned into stories. She has had two novels published by Blue Denim Press: *The Way*

Things Fall (2020), and *In Love With The Night* (2022), and is currently at work on the third in the trilogy. Liz lived and worked in England and Germany before emigrating to Canada, and building a career in advertising and market research. When she is not writing, she will be travelling with her husband to faraway lands.

Juliette Willows (pg. 3) is a writer, self-love advocate, personal growth addict, and flower-child wannabe with a rebel heart. She's an entrepreneur, a seeker of the simple life, and dream-chaser extraordinaire. You'll often find her lost in the depths of her own imagination, silently conjuring magical worlds and secretly wishing they were real. Hailing from the land of the overly-apologetic, she's a Northern girl through and through. Come along with her on a chaotic journey through pages filled with tales of unimaginable creatures, undying love, mysterious strangers, dangerous twists and turns, and a healthy sprinkling of real-life tossed in for good measure.

Ronald Zajac (pg. 23) was born and raised in Montreal, where he completed a B.A. and M.A. in English Literature at McGill University. His work has previously been published in *Matrix, Blank Spaces, The New Quarterly* and the Chicken House Press anthology *The Things We Leave Behind.* He is currently working on a novel and story cycle. He works as a journalist in Brockville, Ontario, cornering the devil in the details, and finding God in the stories they reveal. He would like to save civilization from social media, but admits that is a bit of a stretch goal.

Other Canadian Short Story Anthologies
from Chicken House Press:

The Things We Leave Behind (2022)
Small Town Summer Nights (2023)

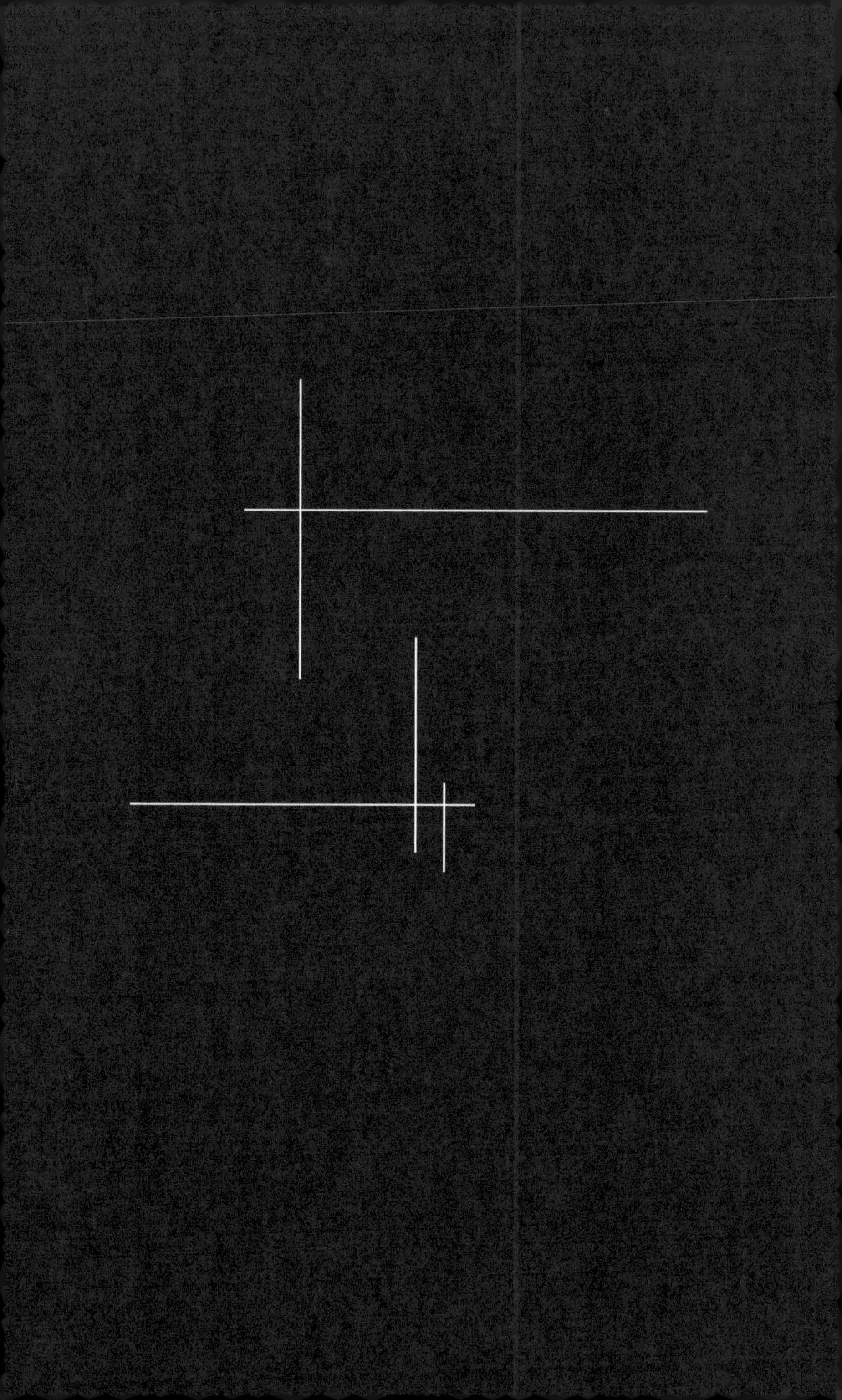